Published By Robert Corbin

@ Omar Noda

Revamp Your Life With Clean Eating: Your

Ultimate Guide to Shredding Belly Fat

All Right RESERVED

ISBN 978-87-94477-14-7

TABLE OF **CONTENTS**

Smoothie With Gleaming Green Spinach And Lettuce 1

Smoothie With Spinach And Collard Greens For Energy.. 3

Avocado And Egg Toast 4

Quinoa And Chickpea Salad 5

Grilled Chicken With Vegetables 7

Apple Ginger Juice 9

Strawberry-Kiwi Juice 10

Veggie Scramble With Mushrooms, Spinach And Goat Cheese 12

Smoked Salmon Boursin Frittata 14

Smoothie Bowl 17

Mushroom Baked Eggs With Squished Tomatoes 19

Sweet Red Pepper Soup 21

Zero Belly Coconut Flour Tortillas 23

Mediterranean Salad-Wraps 25

Ginger Water 27

Green Goddess Salad With Chickpeas 29

Vegan Grain Bowl 31

Spinach And Pineapple Smoothie 33

Kale And Apple Smoothie 34

Greek Yogurt Parfait 36

Veggie Omelette 38

Minty Papaya Green Smoothie 40

Smoothie With Green Pia Colada 41

Green Kiwi Smoothie 42

Chickpea And Kale Salad 44

Green Smoothie 46

Mango-Pineapple Juice 47

Watermelon-Lime Juice 48

Healthy Muffin-Tin Quiches With Smoked Gouda And Ham 50

Protein-Packed Blueberry Lemon Ricotta Pancakes 52

Apple & Sultana Porridge 54

Cardamom & Peach Quinoa Porridge 55

Zero Belly Homemade Baked Beans 57

Zero Belly Mexican Scramble 59

Vietnamese Beef Salad 61

Low-Fat Frittata 64

Avocado Hummus 67

Berry-Kefir Smoothie 69

Cucumber And Mint Smoothie 70

Green Detox Smoothie 72

Blueberry Muffins 74

Turkey And Cheese Lettuce Wraps 79

Smoothie With Mint And Greens 81

Smoothie With Avocado And Lime 82

Detox Water For A Flat Belly 84

Salad-Wraps 85

Peach-Raspberry Juice 87

Pineapple-Orange Juice 89

Homemade Cranberry-Orange Granola 90

Raspberry Peach Swirled Smoothies 93

Peppers & Chickpeas With Tofu 95

Gingerbread Pancakes 98

Oat And Almond Snack Bites 99

Vegetable Scramble 101

Butternut Squash, Tomato, Chard & Chickpea Soup ... 103

Vegetarian Weight Loss Meal Plan 106

Avocado & Smoked Salmon Omelet 109

Red Pepper-Scallion Corn Muffin 111

Hearty Roast Beef Panini 114

Baked Salmon With Roasted Vegetables 122

Smoothie With Tropical Kale And Greens 124

Summer Salad Smoothie 126

Ginger Water Recipe Flat Belly Diet 128

Vietnamese Beef Salad 130

Blueberry-Pomegranate Juice 133

Grapefruit-Cucumber Juice 135

Cali Khichi 136

Fat Flush Soup Recipe 139

Smoothie with gleaming green spinach and lettuce

Ingredients:

- ½ cup diced apples (about ½ medium-sized whole)
- ¼ cup pear dice (about 1 medium-sized whole)
- ½ cup banana slices
- ½ tbsp fresh lemon juice
- 3 cups romaine lettuce, chopped (or about 1 head)
- 2 cups spinach leaves, chopped (about half of a large bunch)
- ½ cup celery, sliced
- 1 cup of water

Directions:

1. Thoroughly wash all veggies and fruits before handling them.
2. Combine the romaine lettuce, spinach, and water in a blender. A process on low speed until the mixture is smooth.
3. Stir in the celery, apple, and pear. The mixture should be blended at high speed.
4. Finally, purée the banana and lemon juice until fully combined.
5. Pour into glasses and serve immediately.

Smoothie with Spinach and Collard Greens for Energy

Ingredients:

- 1 cup spinach, fresh

- 1 cup collard greens, fresh

- 4 medium-sized oranges, whole 3 cups chunked pineapple

Directions:

1. Squeeze the oranges to get the juice. Blend the spinach and collard greens with this fresh juice on a liquid basis. Mix until smooth on low speed.
2. Blend the pineapples into the orange and greens mixture quickly until fully combined.
3. Pour and serve right away.

Avocado and Egg Toast

Ingredients:

- 2 large eggs
- Salt and pepper to taste
- 1/4 tsp paprika (optional)
- 2 slices of whole wheat bread
- 1/2 ripe avocado

Directions:

1. Toast the bread in a toaster or in a pan.
2. Mash the avocado with a fork and spread it over the toast.
3. Fry the eggs in a non-stick pan until the whites are cooked and the yolks are still runny.
4. Place the eggs on top of the avocado toast and season with salt, pepper, and paprika.

Quinoa and Chickpea Salad

Ingredients:

- 1/2 red onion, chopped
- 1/2 red bell pepper, chopped
- 1/4 cup fresh parsley, chopped
- Juice of 1 lemon
- 2 tbsp extra-virgin olive oil
- 1 cup cooked quinoa
- 1 cup cooked chickpeas
- 1/2 cucumber, chopped
- Salt and pepper to taste

Directions:

1. In a large bowl, mix together the quinoa, chickpeas, cucumber, red onion, red bell pepper, and parsley.
2. In a small bowl, whisk together the lemon juice, olive oil, salt, and pepper.
3. Pour the dressing over the salad and toss to combine.
4. Serve chilled.

Grilled Chicken with Vegetables

Ingredients:

- 1 red bell pepper, sliced
- 1 tbsp extra-virgin olive oil
- 1 tsp dried oregano
- 4 boneless, skinless chicken breasts
- 1 zucchini, sliced
- 1 yellow squash, sliced
- Salt and pepper to taste

Directions:

1. Preheat the grill to medium-high heat.
2. Brush the chicken breasts with olive oil and season with oregano, salt, and pepper.
3. Grill the chicken for 5-7 minutes on each side, or until fully cooked.

4. In a separate bowl, mix together the sliced vegetables with olive oil, salt, and pepper.
5. Grill the vegetables for 2-3 minutes on each side, or until tender.
6. Serve the grilled chicken with the vegetables on the side.

Apple Ginger Juice

Ingredients:

- ½ lemon (juiced)
- 1 teaspoon of honey (optional)
- 500ml of sparkling water
- 400g of fresh apples
- 50g of fresh ginger

Directions:

1. The apples should be cleaned and diced.
2. For ginger, it is necessary to peel and cut it into tiny pieces.
3. Juice the apples and ginger together in a Juicer.
4. Add the sparkling water and mix well.
5. As soon as the juice is ready, transfer it into a glass and provide it immediately.

Strawberry-Kiwi Juice

Ingredients:

- 500ml of water

- 1 teaspoon of honey (optional)

- 200g of fresh strawberries

- 200g of fresh kiwis

Directions:

1. Wash and hull the strawberries. Peel and dice the kiwis.
2. In a Juicer, add the strawberries, kiwis, water, and honey (if using).
3. Juice on high speed until the combination is smooth and well combined.
4. If desired, taste and adjust sweetness with additional honey.
5. Filter the juice through a fine-mesh strainer to remove any solids.

6. Transfer the juice to a pitcher or individual glasses.
7. Serve chilled and enjoy.

Veggie Scramble With Mushrooms, Spinach and Goat Cheese

Ingredients:

- 1 cup frozen spinach, thawed
- Salt and black pepper to taste
- 8 eggs
- 2 Tbsp 2% milk
- 1 1/2 Tbsp butter
- 1 cup sliced shiitake mushrooms
- 1/2 cup fresh goat cheese

Directions:

1. Heat 1 tablespoon of the butter in a large nonstick pan over medium heat.
2. When bubbling, add the shiitakes and cook for about 5 minutes, until lightly browned.

3. Remove and reserve on a plate. In the same pan, sauté the spinach until heated all the way through. Season with salt and pepper.
4. Transfer to a colander and squeeze out any excess water.
5. Combine the eggs and the milk in a large bowl.
6. Season with salt and whisk thoroughly. Add the remaining 1/2 tablespoon butter to the pan, turn the heat to low, and add the eggs.
7. Use a wooden spoon to stir the eggs constantly, scraping the bottom of the pan to create small, delicate curds.
8. Continue stirring in this manner for about 5 minutes, until the eggs are still very soft and loose.
9. Add the mushrooms, spinach, and goat cheese and cook for about 2 minutes longer.
10. Season to taste with black pepper.

Smoked salmon boursin frittata

Ingredients:

- ½ tsp pepper
- ¼ cup diced red onion
- 1 (4.4-oz package light Boursin cheese with herbs, softened)
- 2 oz smoked salmon, chopped
- 1 Tbsp extra-virgin olive oil
- Chopped fresh chives
- 6 large eggs
- 2 Tbsp 2% milk
- ¼ cup light sour cream
- 1 tsp kosher salt
- Mesclun salad dressed with vinaigrette

Directions:

1. Preheat oven to 375°F. Position rack in the center of the oven.
2. Whisk the eggs, milk, sour cream, salt, pepper, and red onion together in a bowl.
3. Using two spoons or your fingers, separate the cheese into small clumps. Fold the cheese and salmon into the egg mixture.
4. Heat the oil in a medium ovenproof nonstick skillet over medium-low heat.
5. Pour the egg mixture into the skillet, and stir lightly to make sure the fillings are evenly arranged in the pan.
6. Cook until the bottom is set, but not brown, about 2 minutes.
7. Transfer the skillet to the oven and bake until the top is set, about 8 minutes. Remove from the oven, cover, and set aside for 5 minutes.

8. Invert the frittata onto a large plate. Sprinkle with fresh chives. Cut into wedges and serve warm or at room temperature with salad.

Smoothie bowl

Ingredients:

- 1 tsp maple syrup

- ½ tbsp vanilla protein powder, vegan version if needed

- sliced kiwis, bananas and fresh berries

- 25g granola

- 1 tbsp mixed nuts and seeds

- 200g frozen mixed berries

- 1 ripe banana

- 75ml oat milk

- 1 tbsp almond butter

Directions:

1. Put the berries, banana, oat milk, maple syrup and protein powder in a powerful blender and blend until smooth.
2. Add a splash more milk if needed, but remember it needs to be quite thick.
3. Spoon the smoothie into a bowl and dot over the fresh fruit, granola and mixed nuts and seeds. Drizzle over the almond butter to serve.

Mushroom baked eggs with squished tomatoes

Ingredients:

- a few thyme leaves

- 2 tomatoes, halved

- 2 large eggs

- 2 handfuls rocket

- 2 large flat mushrooms (about 85g each), stalks removed and chopped

- rapeseed oil, for brushing

- ½ garlic clove, grated (optional)

Directions:

1. Heat oven to 200C/180C fan/gas 6. Brush the mushrooms with a little oil and the garlic (if using).

2. Place the mushrooms in two very lightly greased gratin dishes, bottom-side up, and season lightly with pepper.
3. Top with the chopped stalks and thyme, cover with foil and bake for 20 mins.
4. Remove the foil, add the tomatoes to the dishes and break an egg carefully onto each of the mushrooms.
5. Season and add a little more thyme, if you like. Return to the oven for 10-12 mins or until the eggs are set but the yolks are still runny.
6. Top with the rocket and eat straight from the dishes.

Sweet Red Pepper Soup

Ingredients:

- 1 oz almond nut-butter
- 1 medium sweet potato, peeled, chopped
- 2 pints of vegetable broth
- 1 cup of coconut milk
- 1 onion, chopped
- 3 red sweet peppers, chopped
- 1 clove of garlic, minced
- 1 tbsp. coconut oil

Directions:

1. Sweat the onions in the coconut oil for 5 minutes
2. Add everything else except the coconut milk
3. Simmer for 25 minutes

4. Allow to cool slightly then liquidize, adding the coconut milk at this point. Serve immediately

Zero Belly Coconut Flour Tortillas

Ingredients:

- ¼ tsp. of ground kosher sea salt

- 16 egg whites, free-range

- ¾ cup of almond milk

- ½ a cup of coconut flour

- ½ a tsp. of wheat-free baking powder

Directions:

1. Mix all of these Ingredients: in a stainless steel or glass bowl.
2. Let the mix sit for around 10 minutes so that the coconut flour absorbs much of the moisture, and then whisk the mix again.
3. The tortilla batter should ideally be runnier than that of a pancake mix.

4. Heat up a non-stick skillet over a medium to high heat and spray with extra-virgin oil to coat the bottom and sides of the skillet.
5. Pour a ¼ of a cup of the batter into the skillet and give the skillet a swirl so that the tortilla is thin.
6. Once the bottom is done, use a rubber spatula to release the edges of the tortilla then turn it over. When done plate the tortilla.
7. Spray the skillet again and repeat the steps until your batter is used up.

MEDITERRANEAN SALAD-WRAPS

Ingredients:

- 1/2 cup roasted red pepper (blotted dry, drained and sliced)

- 1/4 cucumber, med seedless, halved and thinly sliced (1/2 c)

- 1/2 small red onion, thinly sliced (1/4 c, or sweet onion)

- 2 ounces goat cheese, crumbled

- 1/2 cup green olive tapenade (MUFA)

- 2 tablespoons fresh lemon juice (about 1 lemon)

- 4 cups salad greens (4 oz)

- 1/2 cup chickpeas, rinsed and drained, canned no-salt-added

- 4 tortillas (8-inch diameter) or 4 whole-wheat wraps (8-inch diameter)

Directions:

1. Mix tapenade and lemon juice in large bowl with fork. Add greens, chickpeas, peppers, cucumber, and onion, and toss to mix well. Add cheese and toss gently.
2. Warm wraps or tortillas per package Directions:.
3. Arrange one-quarter of the salad mixture onto the bottom of a wrap and roll up. Cut in half on an angle, placing a wooden pick in each half. Repeat with remaining wraps.

Ginger Water

Ingredients:

- 2 inch ginger root - knob, fresh

- 1 lemon - large

- 1 liter water - plain drinking

Directions:

1. In a large glass jar add in plain water, peeled and grated ginger root and sliced lemons.
2. Stir in all the additions into the water so that they don't settle at the bottom of the jar.
3. Cover the jar with a lid and allow this water to be infused with all the goodness of the ginger and lemons.
4. Allow to steep at least for 6 hours, but overnight is preferred. You may refrigerate the jar of water as well.

5. The next morning pour out the water into a drinking glass, and drink instead of plain water or high calorie sodas.
6. You can use the same Ingredients: by changing the water two times, after which, discard the grated ginger and lemon slices and make a fresh batch.
7. Your ginger water recipe flat belly diet is ready.

Green Goddess Salad with Chickpeas

Ingredients:

Dressing

- ¼ cup chopped fresh herbs, such as tarragon, sorrel, mint, parsley and/or cilantro

- 2 tablespoons rice vinegar

- ½ teaspoon salt

- 1 avocado, peeled and pitted

- 1 ½ cups buttermilk

Salad

- 1 (15 ounce) can chickpeas, rinsed

- ¼ cup diced low-fat Swiss cheese

- 6 cherry tomatoes, halved if desired

- 3 cups chopped romaine lettuce

- 1 cup sliced cucumber

Directions:

1. To prepare dressing: Place avocado, buttermilk, herbs, vinegar and salt in a blender. Puree until smooth.
2. To prepare salad: Toss lettuce and cucumber in a bowl with 1/4 cup of the dressing. Top with chickpeas, cheese and tomatoes. (Refrigerate the extra dressing for up to 3 days.)

Vegan Grain Bowl

Ingredients:

- 1 tablespoon lemon juice

- 1 small clove garlic, minced

- 2 cups cooked quinoa

- 1 15-ounce can chickpeas, rinsed

- 1 firm ripe avocado, diced

- ¼ cup chopped fresh cilantro or parsley

- 1 medium sweet potato, peeled if desired, cut into 1-inch chunks

- 3 tablespoons extra-virgin olive oil, divided

- ½ teaspoon salt, divided

- ½ teaspoon ground pepper, divided

- 2 tablespoons tahini

- 2 tablespoons water

Directions:

1. Preheat oven to 425 degrees F.
2. Toss sweet potato with 1 tablespoon oil and 1/4 teaspoon each salt and pepper in a medium bowl.
3. Transfer to a rimmed baking sheet. Roast, stirring once, until tender, 15 to 18 minutes.
4. Meanwhile, whisk the remaining 2 tablespoons oil, tahini, water, lemon juice, garlic and the remaining 1/4 teaspoon each salt and pepper in a small bowl.
5. To serve, divide quinoa among 4 bowls. Top with equal amounts of sweet potato, chickpeas and avocado.
6. Drizzle with the tahini sauce. Sprinkle with parsley (or cilantro).

Spinach and pineapple smoothie

Ingredients:

- 1 banana
- 1 cup coconut water
- 1 tsp honey (optional)
- 2 cups fresh spinach
- 1 cup chopped fresh or frozen pineapple

Directions:

1. Add the fresh spinach to a blender.
2. Add the chopped pineapple, banana, coconut water, and honey (if using).
3. Blend all the Ingredients: until it becomes smooth and creamy.
4. If the smoothie is too thick, add a little more coconut water or water to thin it out.
5. Pour into glasses and serve.

Kale and apple smoothie

Ingredients:

- 1 cup of unsweetened almond milk
- 1/2 teaspoon of grated ginger
- 1 tablespoon of chia seeds
- 1 teaspoon of honey (optional)
- 2 cups of fresh kale leaves, chopped
- 1 medium-sized apple, cored and sliced
- 1 frozen banana, sliced
- Ice cubes (optional)

Directions:

1. Wash the kale leaves and chop them into small pieces.
2. Core the apple and slice it into small pieces.

3. Slice the frozen banana.
4. Add the kale, apple, frozen banana, grated ginger, chia seeds, and almond milk to a blender.
5. Blend until the Ingredients: are smooth and creamy.
6. Taste the smoothie and add honey, if desired.
7. If the smoothie is too thick, add ice cubes and blend again until it reaches the desired consistency.
8. Pour the smoothie into a glass and enjoy!

Greek Yogurt Parfait

Ingredients:

- 1/4 cup granola

- 1 tsp honey (optional)

- 1 cup Greek yogurt

- 1/2 cup fresh berries (such as strawberries, blueberries, or raspberries)

DIRECTIONS:

1. In a small bowl, mix together the Greek yogurt and honey (if using) until well combined.
2. In a separate bowl, rinse and chop your fresh berries.
3. Layer the Greek yogurt mixture, berries, and granola in a glass or jar, starting with a layer of yogurt at the bottom.

4. Continue layering the yogurt, berries, and granola until you reach the top of the glass or jar.
5. Serve immediately or store in the refrigerator for later.

Veggie Omelette

Ingredients:

- 1/4 cup chopped vegetables (such as bell peppers, onions, spinach, mushrooms, or tomatoes)

- 1/4 cup shredded cheese

- Salt and pepper to taste

- 2 eggs

- 1 tbsp olive oil or butter

DIRECTIONS:

1. In a small bowl, whisk together the eggs with salt and pepper.
2. In a nonstick skillet over medium heat, add the olive oil or butter and let it melt.
3. Once the oil or butter is hot, add the chopped vegetables and sauté for a few minutes until they are tender.

4. Pour the whisked eggs into the skillet over the vegetables and let the mixture cook for a few minutes until the eggs start to set.
5. Once the bottom of the omelette is cooked and lightly browned, sprinkle the shredded cheese over the top.
6. Using a spatula, fold one side of the omelette over the other to create a half-moon shape.
7. Let the omelette cook for another minute or so until the cheese is melted and the eggs are fully cooked.
8. Carefully slide the omelette onto a plate and serve hot.

Minty Papaya Green Smoothie

Ingredients:

- 2 cups ripe papaya, diced 1 cup pear cubes 2 teaspoons goji berries (dried or fresh) 10 mint leaves, fresh
- 1 cup purified water
- 3 cups fresh spinach leaves

DIRECTIONS:

1. Fill the blender halfway with water. Then, add the papaya, then the pear, berries, and finally, the mint leaves. Last, add the spinach.
2. Mix on high for 30 seconds or until the smoothie has reached an even and creamy consistency.
3. Serve immediately.

Smoothie with Green Pia Colada

Ingredients:

- ½ cup shredded coconut

- 4 tbsp. of dry pitted dates

- 2 cups coconut water

- 1 cup dandelion greens, chopped

- 4 cups of ripe pineapple chunks

- Unsweetened 2 cups cubed ice

DIRECTIONS:

1. Combine all the Ingredients: in a blender. Remember to put the liquid first, followed by the greens. In between, add Ingredients:.
2. Mix on high until the puree is creamy and smooth.
3. Strain into glasses and serve.

Green Kiwi Smoothie

Ingredients:

- ½ kiwifruit juice
- ½ lemon juice
- 1 cup of purified water
- 1 teaspoon pollen from bees
- 1 cup kale leaves, chopped
- 1 cup Romaine lettuce, chopped
- 1 cup Swiss chard leaves, cut
- ½ cup ripe bananas, sliced
- ½ tsp maca powder

DIRECTIONS:

1. Thoroughly wash all components. Follow the recipe's instructions.

2. Combine all of the Ingredients: in a blender. Mix on high until smooth.
3. Pour into a glass and serve right away.

Chickpea and Kale Salad

Ingredients:

- 2 tbsp. olive oil

- 2 tbsp. lemon juice

- 1 clove garlic, minced

- Salt and pepper to taste

- 1 can chickpeas, drained and rinsed

- 1 bunch kale, stems removed and leaves chopped

- 1/4 cup sliced almonds

- 1/4 cup crumbled feta cheese

DIRECTIONS:

1. In a large bowl, combine the chickpeas, kale, almonds, and feta cheese.

2. In a small bowl, whisk together the olive oil, lemon juice, garlic, salt, and pepper.
3. Drizzle the dressing over the salad and toss to coat.
4. Serve chilled.

Green Smoothie

Ingredients:

- 1/2 avocado

- 1/2 cup unsweetened almond milk

- 1 tbsp chia seeds

- 1 banana

- 1/2 cup frozen spinach

- 1/2 cup frozen pineapple

DIRECTIONS:

1. Combine all Ingredients: in a blender.
2. Blend until smooth and creamy.
3. Serve and enjoy!

Mango-Pineapple Juice

Ingredients:

- 120ml of water
- 1 tablespoon of honey
- Ice cubes
- 150g of mango
- 150g of pineapple

Directions:

1. Place the diced mango, pineapple chunks, water, and honey in a Juicer.
2. Juice on high speed until uniform and well combined.
3. If desired, add ice cubes.
4. Pour the juice into glasses and serve immediately.

Watermelon-Lime Juice

Ingredients:

- 1 tablespoon honey (optional)
- Ice cubes
- 500g watermelon, cubed
- 2 limes (juiced)

Directions:

1. Wash and cube the watermelon, removing any seeds.
2. Squeeze the juice from two limes and set aside.
3. Place the cubed watermelon in a juicer.
4. Add the lime juice and honey (if desired) to the juicer.
5. Juice the watermelon and limes until smooth.
6. Strain the juice to remove any pulp or seeds, if desired.
7. Pour the juice into glasses and add ice cubes.

8. Stir well, and serve immediately.

Healthy Muffin-Tin Quiches With Smoked Gouda and Ham

Ingredients:

- 8 large eggs

- 1 cup shredded smoked Gouda cheese

- ½ cup 2% milk

- ½ teaspoon ground black pepper

- ½ cup diced ham

- 1 (10-oz) package frozen chopped broccoli, thawed and well drained

- Nonstick cooking spray

- 2 Tbsp extra-virgin olive oil

- 1 cup finely diced red-skinned potatoes

- 1 small shallot, minced

- ¾ tsp salt, divided

DIRECTIONS:

1. Preheat oven to 325°F. Coat a 12-cup standard muffin tin with cooking spray.
2. Heat oil in a large skillet over medium heat. Add potatoes, shallot, and ¼ teaspoon salt and cook, stirring, until the potatoes are just cooked through, about 5 minutes. Remove from heat and let cool 5 minutes.
3. Whisk eggs, cheese, milk, pepper, and the remaining ½ teaspoon salt in a large bowl. Stir in ham, broccoli, and the potato mixture.
4. Divide mixture among the prepared muffin cups.
5. Bake for 25 minutes or until firm to the touch. Let stand for 5 minutes before serving.

Protein-Packed Blueberry Lemon Ricotta Pancakes

Ingredients:

- 1 cup plain Greek yogurt

- 1 cup low-fat cottage cheese or ricotta

- 3 eggs

- Juice of 1 lemon

- 1 cup white whole wheat flour (we like King Arthur's, but these can be just as easily made with white flour—you'll just sacrifice a few grams of fiber.)

- 1/2 tsp baking soda

- 2 cups frozen wild blueberries

- 1/2 cup water

- 1/4 cup sugar

- Pinch of salt

DIRECTIONS:

1. Mix the blueberries, water, and sugar in a saucepan.
2. Cook over low heat, stirring often, for 10 minutes or until the blueberries begin to break apart.
3. Whisk together the yogurt, cottage cheese, eggs, and lemon juice in a bowl. Mix the flour, baking soda, and salt in another bowl.
4. Add the flour to the yogurt mixture, and stir just until blended.
5. Heat a large skillet or sauté pan over medium-low heat.
6. Coat with nonstick cooking spray, and add batter in large spoonfuls (about 1/4 cup each).
7. Flip the pancakes when the tops begin to bubble, 3 to 5 minutes, and cook the second side until browned. Serve with the warm blueberries.

Apple & sultana porridge

Ingredients:

- 4 apples, cored and diced
- 100g sultana
- 1 tbsp brown sugar, to serve
- 100g porridge oat
- 500ml skimmed milk

DIRECTIONS:

1. Put the oats and milk in a small pan and cook, stirring, for 3 mins until almost creamy.
2. Stir in the apples and sultanas, then cook for 2 mins more or until the porridge is thick and creamy and the apples just tender.
3. Ladle into bowls, sprinkle with sugar and eat immediately.

Cardamom & peach quinoa porridge

Ingredients:

- 250ml unsweetened almond milk
- 2 ripe peaches, cut into slices
- 1 tsp maple syrup
- 75g quinoa
- 25g porridge oats
- 4 cardamom pods

DIRECTIONS:

1. Put the quinoa, oats and cardamom pods in a small saucepan with 250ml water and 100ml of the almond milk.
2. Bring to the boil, then simmer gently for 15 mins, stirring occasionally.
3. Pour in the remaining almond milk and cook for 5 mins more until creamy.

4. Remove the cardamom pods, spoon into bowls or jars, and top with the peaches and maple syrup.

Zero Belly Homemade Baked Beans

Ingredients:

- 7 oz. Pinto beans, cooked, drained and rinsed

- 7 oz. Kidney beans, cooked, drained, rinsed

- 1 carrot, shredded

- 1 tsp. Of dried cumin powder

- 1 tsp. Of fresh (chopped) or dried oregano

- 1 tsp. Of dried thyme

- ½ Tsp. Of cayenne pepper

- 1 tbsp. Coconut oil

- 1 large yellow onion, peeled and diced

- 1 cup of fresh crushed tomatoes

- 2 cups of grape tomatoes, chopped in half

- Kosher salt and freshly ground black pepper

DIRECTIONS:

1. Heat coconut oil in a skillet over medium heat.
2. Add the chopped onions and cook, stirring, until onions are clear and done.
3. Add all of the tomatoes and simmer for 5 minutes to release their sugary sweetness.
4. Add both types of beans, shredded carrot, spices and herbs then continue to simmer for at least 10 more minutes.
5. Season baked beans with sea salt and freshly cracked pepper.
6. Serve with the zero belly tortillas, enjoy!

Zero Belly Mexican Scramble

Ingredients:

- 2 tbsp. onion, peeled, chopped

- 1 tbsp. red pepper, chopped

- 1 cup of prepared home-made baked beans

- 1 tbsp. of extra-virgin olive oil

- 2 free-range eggs

- Tbsp. coconut cream

- Kosher salt and fresh ground pepper to taste

DIRECTIONS:

1. Whisk the eggs, coconut cream and seasonings together.
2. Heat a skillet with olive oil and sauté the onion and pepper until done.
3. Turn down heat to medium and add the baked beans, heat up and then pour in the

egg mix and stir to mix through and cook until egg mix is done.

4. Plate up and serve with a dollop of home-made salsa. Enjoy!

VIETNAMESE BEEF SALAD

INGREDIENTS:

- 6 cups mixed greens

- 1 cup sweet basil

- 1 cup cilantro leaf

- 1 red onion, thinly sliced (about 1 1/4 cups)

- 2 large English seedless cucumbers, with peel, julienned (about 4 c)

- 4 medium carrots, julienned (about2c)

- 1/4 cup soy sauce, reduced sodium

- 1/4 cup lime juice

- 1/4 cup water

- 2 tablespoons sugar

- 1 tablespoon garlic, minced

- 2 teaspoons chili paste

- 1/2 lb flank steak

- 1/2 cup dry-roasted unsalted peanuts (MUFA, chopped)

DIRECTIONS:

1. COMBINE soy sauce, lime juice, water, sugar, garlic, and chile paste in medium bowl. Whisk to blend. Pour 3 tablespoons into a resealable plastic bag. Cover and refrigerate the remaining dressing. Add steak to bag, seal, and turn to coat. Chill 30 minutes to marinate.
2. HEAT grill or broiler to medium-high heat. Grill steak 8 to 10 minutes, turning once, or until medium-rare. Let rest 5 minutes and slice thinly at an angle, across the grain.
3. PLACE greens, basil, and cilantro in large bowl and toss. Evenly divide mixture among 4 plates. Sprinkle on onion, cucumbers, and carrots. Top with sliced steak, drizzle salad

with reserved dressing, and sprinkle with peanuts.

LOW-FAT FRITTATA

INGREDIENTS:

- 1/4 cup cold water
- 1/2 teaspoon dried tarragon or 1/2
- teaspoon fresh tarragon, finely chopped
- 1/2 teaspoon salt
- 2 ounces smoked salmon, thinly sliced, cut into 1/2-inch-wide pieces
- 3/4 cup tapenade (Black olive, MUFA)
- 2 teaspoons extra virgin olive oil
- 6 scallions, trimmed and chopped (whites and 2-inch of green)
- 6 large egg whites
- 4 large eggs

DIRECTIONS:

1. Preheat oven to 350°F.
2. Heat heavy 8" ovenproof sauté pan over medium heat 1 minute.
3. Add oil and heat 20 seconds.
4. Add scallions and sauté, stirring periodically with spatula, about 2 minutes or until soft.
5. Combine egg whites, eggs, water, tarragon, and salt in medium bowl.
6. Whisk to blend. Season with freshly ground black pepper.
7. Pour mixture into pan and lay salmon on top. Cook, stirring periodically, about 2 minutes or until partially set.
8. Transfer pan to oven and cook 12 to 14 minutes or until firm, golden, and puffed. Remove from oven. Use spatula to release frittata from pan.
9. Gently slide onto warm serving platter, slice, and serve with 2 tablespoons of the tapenade.

10. Make it a Flat Belly Diet Meal.
11. For a well-balanced dish, thaw 1/2 cup of frozen dark sweet cherries (45 calories) and combine with 1 cup of fat-free plain Greek-style yogurt (112 calories). Top with 1/4 cup of toasted whole oats (75 calories).

Avocado Hummus

Ingredients:

- ¼ cup extra-virgin olive oil
- ¼ cup lemon juice
- 1 clove garlic
- 1 teaspoon ground cumin
- ½ teaspoon salt
- 1 (15 ounce) can no-salt-added chickpeas
- 1 ripe avocado, halved and pitted
- 1 cup fresh cilantro leaves
- ¼ cup tahini

Directions:

1. Drain chickpeas, reserving 2 tablespoons of the liquid.

2. Transfer the chickpeas and the reserved liquid to a food processor.
3. Add avocado, cilantro, tahini, oil, lemon juice, garlic, cumin and salt.
4. Puree until very smooth. Serve with veggie chips, pita chips or crudités.

Berry-Kefir Smoothie

Ingredients:

- ½ medium banana

- 2 teaspoons almond butter

- ½ teaspoon vanilla extract

- 1 ½ cups frozen mixed berries

- 1 cup plain kefir

Directions:

1. Combine berries, kefir, banana, almond butter and vanilla in a blender. Blend until smooth.

Cucumber and mint smoothie

Ingredients:

- 1/2 cup of plain Greek yogurt
- 1/2 cup of unsweetened almond milk
- 1 tablespoon of honey (optional)
- Juice of 1/2 lemon
- 2 cups of chopped cucumber
- 1/2 cup of fresh mint leaves
- Ice cubes (optional)

Directions:

1. Wash the cucumber and chop it into small pieces.
2. Wash the mint leaves and remove the stems.
3. Add the cucumber, mint leaves, Greek yogurt, almond milk, and lemon juice to a blender.

4. Blend until the Ingredients: are smooth and creamy.
5. Taste the smoothie and add honey, if desired.
6. If the smoothie is too thick, add ice cubes and blend again until it reaches the desired consistency.
7. Pour the smoothie into a glass and enjoy!

Green detox smoothie

Ingredients:

- 1/2 inch piece of fresh ginger
- 1/2 lemon, juiced
- 1/2 cup unsweetened almond milk
- 1/2 cup water
- 1 tbsp chia seeds
- Ice cubes (optional)
- 1 banana
- 1 cup fresh spinach leaves
- 1/2 cup chopped cucumber
- 1/2 cup chopped pineapple

Directions:

1. Start by washing all the fresh produce thoroughly.
2. Add the banana, spinach, cucumber, pineapple, ginger, lemon juice, almond milk, and water to a blender.
3. Blend on high speed for about 1-2 minutes, or until the mixture is smooth and creamy.
4. If you like your smoothie colder, add a few ice cubes and blend again.
5. Finally, add the chia seeds and blend briefly until they are evenly distributed throughout the smoothie.
6. Pour the smoothie into a tall glass and enjoy!

Blueberry Muffins

Ingredients:

- 1/3 cup vegetable oil
- 1 egg
- 1/3 cup milk
- 1 tsp vanilla extract
- 1 cup fresh blueberries
- 1 1/2 cups all-purpose flour
- 1/2 cup sugar
- 1/2 tsp salt
- 2 tsp baking powder

DIRECTIONS:

1. Preheat your oven to 400°F (200°C) and line a muffin tin with paper liners or grease with cooking spray.

2. In a large mixing bowl, whisk together the flour, sugar, salt, and baking powder.
3. In a separate bowl, mix together the vegetable oil, egg, milk, and vanilla extract.
4. Add the wet Ingredients: to the dry Ingredients: and mix until just combined. Do not overmix.
5. Gently fold in the fresh blueberries, being careful not to crush them.
6. Spoon the batter into the muffin cups, filling each one about 3/4 full.
7. Bake the muffins for 18-20 minutes or until a toothpick inserted in the center comes out clean.
8. Remove the muffins from the oven and let them cool in the tin for 5-10 minutes before transferring to a wire rack to cool completely.
9. Serve the blueberry muffins warm or at room temperature.

Avocado Toast with Poached Eggs

Ingredients:

- Salt and pepper to taste

- 1 tbsp white vinegar

- 1 tbsp olive oil or butter

- 2 slices of bread

- 1 ripe avocado

- 2 eggs

DIRECTIONS:

1. Toast the bread to your desired level of doneness and set aside.
2. Cut the avocado in half and remove the pit. Scoop out the flesh and mash it with a fork in a small bowl. Add salt and pepper to taste.

3. Fill a medium saucepan with water and bring it to a simmer over medium heat. Add the white vinegar and stir.
4. Crack one egg into a small bowl. Using a spoon, stir the simmering water in the saucepan in one direction to create a whirlpool.
5. Carefully pour the egg into the center of the whirlpool and let it cook for 3-4 minutes, or until the whites are set but the yolk is still runny.
6. Use a slotted spoon to remove the poached egg from the water and place it on a paper towel to drain excess water. Repeat with the second egg.
7. Spread the mashed avocado on top of each slice of toast.
8. Place a poached egg on top of the avocado on each slice of toast.

9. Drizzle with olive oil or melted butter and sprinkle with salt and pepper to taste.
10. Serve immediately and enjoy your delicious avocado toast with poached eggs.

Turkey and Cheese Lettuce Wraps

Ingredients:

- 1/2 avocado, sliced
- 1/2 red onion, thinly sliced
- 1/2 red bell pepper, thinly sliced
- 1/4 cup mayonnaise
- 1 tbsp Dijon mustard
- 4 large lettuce leaves
- 4-6 slices of turkey breast
- 4 slices of your preferred cheese (cheddar, Swiss, or pepper jack)
- Salt and pepper to taste

DIRECTIONS:

1. Wash and dry the lettuce leaves and set them aside.

2. In a small bowl, mix together the mayonnaise and Dijon mustard to make the sauce.
3. Place a slice of cheese on top of each lettuce leaf.
4. Layer the turkey slices on top of the cheese.
5. Add sliced avocado, red onion, and red bell pepper on top of the turkey.
6. Drizzle the sauce over the filling.
7. Season with salt and pepper to taste.
8. Roll up the lettuce leaves tightly to create a wrap.
9. Serve immediately and enjoy your delicious turkey and cheese lettuce wraps.

Smoothie with Mint and Greens

Ingredients:

- 2 tbsp. raw cashew butter

- 1 litre of distilled water

- 1 cup spinach leaves, chopped

- 10 fresh mint leaves

- 2 pitted dates in their entirety

DIRECTIONS:

1. Combine all the Ingredients: in a blender. Whizz on high until smooth.
2. Pour into glasses and serve right away.

Smoothie with Avocado and Lime

Ingredients:

- ½ cup cucumber slices

- ½ avocado (fruit) 3 limes, whole

- 1 cup spinach leaves, young

- Sweetener of choice (honey, agave, or stevia) six pieces cubes of ice

DIRECTIONS:

1. Thoroughly wash all veggies and fruits.
2. Remove the leaves from the spinach. Remove the stems.
3. Cut the cucumber into half-inch pieces without peeling.
4. Remove the avocado seed. Scoop out the meat from the peeling using a spoon.
5. Peel and cut limes into quarters.

6. Combine cucumber, avocado, spinach, and lime in a blender. Add ice cubes and sweetener to taste.
7. Mix all of the Ingredients: until smooth.
8. Pour into a glass and serve immediately.
9. To add zest to your smoothie, add ½ tsp cinnamon powder.

Detox Water for a Flat Belly

Ingredients:

- 1 tbsp. ginger, grated

- 1 cucumber, sliced

- 1 lemon, sliced

- 6 c filtered water

- 1/3 c mint leaves

DIRECTIONS:

1. Mix all of the Ingredients: together in a pitcher and store it in the fridge overnight, so that the flavors can infuse.
2. Drink it all the next day. It will help flush fat from your body.

SALAD-WRAPS

INGREDIENTS:

- 1/2 cup roasted red pepper (blotted dry, drained and sliced)

- 1/4 cucumber, med seedless, halved and thinly sliced (1/2 c)

- 1/2 small red onion, thinly sliced (1/4 c, or sweet onion)

- 2 ounces goat cheese, crumbled

- 1/2 cup green olive tapenade (MUFA)

- 2 tablespoons fresh lemon juice (about 1 lemon)

- 4 cups salad greens (4 oz)

- 1/2 cup chickpeas, rinsed and drained, canned no-salt-added

- 4 tortillas (8-inch diameter) or 4 whole-wheat wraps (8-inch diameter)

DIRECTIONS:

1. Mix tapenade and lemon juice in large bowl with fork.
2. Add greens, chickpeas, peppers, cucumber, and onion, and toss to mix well. Add cheese and toss gently.
3. Warm wraps or tortillas per package Directions:.
4. Arrange one-quarter of the salad mixture onto the bottom of a wrap and roll up.
5. Cut in half on an angle, placing a wooden pick in each half. Repeat with remaining wraps.

Peach-Raspberry Juice

Ingredients:

- 120ml of water

- 1 tablespoon of honey (optional)

- Ice cubes (optional)

- 200g of fresh peaches

- 150g of fresh raspberry

Directions:

1. Clean and peel the peaches, remove the pit, and chop them into small pieces.
2. Rinse the raspberries, then add them to the diced peaches in a juicer.
3. Juice the Ingredients: until smooth.
4. Add water and mix well.
5. If desired, strain the mixture to get rid of any pulp or seeds using a fine-mesh screen.

6. You may either serve the juice now or store it in the fridge.

Pineapple-Orange Juice

Ingredients:

- 200 grams of fresh pineapple

- 100 grams of fresh oranges

Directions:

1. Slice up the pineapple after peeling it.
2. Oranges should be seedless and peeled.
3. Juice the pineapple and oranges in a juicer until they are well combined.
4. Serve the juice immediately by pouring it into a glass.

Homemade Cranberry-Orange Granola

Ingredients:

- ½ cup orange juice

- 2 Tbsp pure maple syrup

- 2 tsp orange zest

- ½ tsp pumpkin pie spice

- ½ cup dried cranberries

- Fat-free milk, nonfat yogurt, or fresh fruit (optional) Nonstick cooking spray

- 2 ½ cups regular rolled oats

- 1 cup wheat flakes

- 1/3 cup whole bran cereal such as Grape-Nuts

- 1/3 cup coarsely chopped pecans

DIRECTIONS:

1. Preheat oven to 325°F. Coat a 15 x 10 x 1-inch pan with nonstick cooking spray or line with parchment paper; set aside.
2. In a large bowl, stir together oats, wheat flakes, bran cereal, and pecans.
3. In a small saucepan, stir together orange juice, maple syrup, orange zest, and pumpkin pie spice. Cook and stir just until boiling.
4. Remove from heat. Pour over oat mixture; toss just until coated.
5. Spread oat mixture evenly in prepared pan. Bake for 30 to 35 minutes, or until oats are lightly browned, stirring twice. Remove from oven and stir in dried cranberries.
6. Immediately turn out onto a large piece of foil; cool completely.
7. Serve with milk or use to make a breakfast parfait with nonfat yogurt and fresh fruit.

8. Store in an airtight container in the refrigerator for up to 2 weeks or in the freezer for up to 3 months.

Raspberry peach swirled smoothies

Ingredients:

- 1 ½ cups frozen peach slices

- 1 ripe banana, cut into 2-inch chunks and frozen for at least 2 hours

- 1 Tbsp honey

- ¼ tsp ground ginger

- ½ cup frozen unsweetened raspberries, thawed

- 1/3 cup orange juice

- 2 5.3-oz cartons nonfat vanilla Greek yogurt

- Fresh raspberries (optional)

DIRECTIONS:

1. In a blender, combine raspberries and orange juice. Cover and blend until smooth. Divide between two glasses.

2. Wash out the blender. In the clean blender, combine yogurt, peaches, banana, honey, and ginger. Cover and blend until smooth.
3. Pour over raspberry mixture in glasses.
4. Swirl with a spoon. If desired, top with fresh raspberries. Serve immediately.

peppers & chickpeas with tofu

Ingredients:

- 2 tsp vegetable bouillon powder

- 1 tsp dried oregano

- 1 tsp smoked paprika, plus extra for sprinkling

- 2 x 400g cans chickpeas

- 280g pack extra-firm tofu

- 240g soya yogurt

- 2 garlic cloves, finely grated

- 4 tbsp chopped parsley

- 1-2 tbsp olive oil

- 2 onions (320g), halved and thinly sliced

- 1 orange pepper, halved, deseeded and sliced

- 1 red chilli, deseeded and sliced

- 400g can chopped tomatoes

- 2 tbsp tomato purée

DIRECTIONS:

1. Heat 1 tbsp oil in a large, deep frying pan over a medium heat.
2. Tip in the onions, cover and cook for 5 mins. Remove the lid and stir the onions – they should have softened and started to brown in places.
3. Stir in the pepper, chilli, chopped tomatoes, tomato purée, bouillon powder, oregano, paprika and chickpeas, along with the liquid from the cans. Cover and simmer for 15-20 mins until slightly thickened.
4. Meanwhile, slice half the tofu and fry in ½ tbsp oil over a medium heat until lightly golden. Combine the yogurt and garlic in a small bowl.
5. If you're following the Healthy Diet Plan, serve half the tomato and chickpea mixture with the

tofu, half the yogurt and a scattering of parsley and extra paprika.

Gingerbread pancakes

Ingredients:

- ½ tbsp maple syrup, plus extra to serve

- 200ml full-fat milk or semi-skimmed milk

- vegetable oil, for frying

- 100g pitted dates, chopped, to serve

- 100ml crème fraîche, to serve

- 150g self-raising flour

- ½ tsp baking powder

- 1 tsp ground ginger

- 1 tsp cinnamon

- 2 tsp golden caster sugar

- 1 egg, beaten

DIRECTIONS:

1. Put the flour, baking powder, ginger, cinnamon and sugar in a large bowl with a pinch of salt.
2. Combine the egg, maple syrup and milk in a jug.
3. Gradually add to the dry Ingredients:, whisking until a smooth, silky batter forms.
4. Heat a drizzle of oil in a large, non-stick pan over a medium heat and ladle 2-3 small rounds into the pan.
5. Cook for 1-2 mins until bubbles start to appear on the surface, then flip over and cook for a further 1 min until fluffy. Do this in batches until you have 10 pancakes.
6. Serve in a stack, with extra maple syrup, a blob of crème fraîche and dates scattered over.

Oat and Almond Snack Bites

Ingredients:

- 1 tbsp. Protein powder

- ½ cup of rolled oats, gluten-free

- 1 cup of home-made almond butter (or natural bought)

- ½ Cup of coconut milk

DIRECTIONS:

1. In a microwave bowl combine almond butter and coconut milk. Zap for around 2 minutes or until almond butter is easily spread.
2. Remove the bowl from microwave and stir until combined
3. Stir in the protein powder and keep stirring until it is completely dissolved and mixed.
4. Add the oats and stir to mix.
5. Roll the mix into bite-size circles and refrigerate for 15-20 minutes until the bites are hardened.
6. Eat with fresh fruit for breakfast or as snacks.

Vegetable Scramble

Ingredients:

- ¼ Cup green bell pepper, chopped

- Cup of chopped cherry tomatoes

- 6 free-range eggs

- ¼ cup coconut milk

- ¼ Cup of extra-virgin olive oil

- ¼ Cup mushrooms, sliced

- ¼ Cup onions, peeled, chopped

DIRECTIONS:

1. Heat the extra-virgin olive oil in a skillet over medium-high heat.
2. Add the sliced mushrooms, onions and bell pepper; sauté until the onions are transparent.

3. In a large bowl, beat together eggs and coconut milk.
4. Add the mixture to the vegetables; stir in tomatoes.
5. Cook until the eggs are done. Serve immediately.

Butternut Squash, Tomato, Chard & Chickpea Soup

Ingredients:

- 3 teaspoons finely chopped garlic

- 1 ½ teaspoons finely chopped fresh ginger

- 1 teaspoon ground turmeric

- ½ teaspoon ground cumin

- ½ teaspoon salt

- 6 cups low-sodium vegetable broth

- 1 (15 ounce) can no-salt-added stewed tomatoes

- 3 cups stemmed and chopped rainbow chard

- 1 (15 ounce) can unsalted chickpeas, rinsed

- 1 tablespoon extra-virgin olive oil

- 2 cups chopped butternut squash

- 1 cup chopped onion

- ¾ cup sliced parsnips (1/3-inch)

- 1 tablespoon cider vinegar

- 1 tablespoon chopped fresh flat-leaf parsley

DIRECTIONS:

1. Heat oil in a large heavy pot over medium-high heat.
2. Add squash, onion and parsnips; cook, stirring occasionally, until starting to soften, about 5 minutes.
3. Add garlic, ginger, turmeric, cumin and salt; cook, stirring constantly, until fragrant, about 1 minute.
4. Add broth and tomatoes; bring to a boil. Reduce heat to medium; simmer until the vegetables are tender, 8 to 10 minutes.

5. Add chard and chickpeas; cook, stirring occasionally, until the chard is bright green and starting to soften, about 2 minutes.
6. Remove from heat; stir in vinegar. Sprinkle with parsley and serve immediately.

Vegetarian Weight Loss Meal Plan

INGREDIENTS:

- 1 cup brown lentils, cooked (1 cup = 1/ 15oz / 235g lentils or a 400g can)

- 1 handful arugula/rocket (1 handful = 100 g)

- 2 tbsp balsamic vinegar

- Salt and pepper to taste

- 1 small handful raisins

- ½ cup cashews (½ cups = 75 g)

- 1 onion

- 1 tsp olive oil

- 1 chili / jalapeño

- 4 sun-dried tomatoes in oil

- 3 slice wholegrain bread (whole wheat)

- 1 tsp maple syrup

DIRECTIONS:

1. Roast the cashews on a low heat for about three minutes in a pan to maximize aroma. Then throw them into the salad bowl. ½ cup cashews
2. Dice up and fry the onion in olive oil for about 3 minutes on a low heat. 1 onion, 1 tsp olive oil
3. Move the onion mix into a big bowl.
4. Meanwhile chop the chilli/jalapeño and dried tomatoes.
5. Cut the bread into big croutons. Add them to the pan and fry for another 2 minutes until the bread is crunchy.
6. The oil from the sun-dried tomatoes should do.1 chili / jalapeño, 4 sun-dried tomatoes in oil, 3 slice wholegrain bread
7. Season with salt and pepper.Salt and pepper to taste

8. Wash the arugula and add it to the bowl. Add the raisins. 1 handful arugula/rocket, 1 small handful raisins
9. Put the lentils in too. Season with salt, pepper, maple syrup and balsamic vinegar. Finally, serve with the croutons mix. 1 cup brown lentils, cooked, 1 tsp maple syrup, 2 tbsp balsamic vinegar
10. Super tasty!

Avocado & Smoked Salmon Omelet

Ingredients:

- Pinch of salt

- 1 teaspoon extra-virgin olive oil plus 1/2 teaspoon, divided

- ¼ avocado, sliced

- 1 ounce smoked salmon

- 2 large eggs

- 1 teaspoon low-fat milk

- 1 tablespoon chopped fresh basil

Directions:
1. Beat eggs with milk and salt in a small bowl. Heat 1 teaspoon oil in a small nonstick skillet over medium heat.

2. Add the egg mixture and cook until the bottom is set and the center is still a bit runny, 1 to 2 minutes.
3. Flip the omelet over and cook until set, about 30 seconds more.
4. Transfer to a plate. Top with avocado, salmon and basil. Drizzle with the remaining 1/2 teaspoon oil.

Red Pepper-Scallion Corn Muffin

Ingredients:

- 1/2 c whole grain pastry flour
- 1¾ tsp baking powder
- 1/2 tsp salt
- 1/4 tsp baking soda
- 1/8 tsp freshly ground black pepper
- 1 c fat-free plain yogurt
- 1 large egg
- 2 large egg whites
- 2 tsp brown sugar
- 2 Tbsp + 1/4 c canola oil, divided
- 1 large red bell pepper, coarsely chopped
- 4 scallions, thinly sliced

- 1½ c yellow cornmeal

- 3/4 c drained canned vacuum-packed corn kernels (about 1/2 an 11-ounce can)

Directions:
1. PREHEAT oven to 350°F. Coat Texas-size, 6-cup muffin tin with cooking spray or line with paper baking cups.
2. WARM 2 Tbsp of the oil in medium skillet over medium heat. Add bell pepper and cook, stirring, 5 minutes or until tender.
3. Add scallions. Cook, stirring, 1 minute or until softened. Remove from heat and let cool 5 minutes.
4. STIR together cornmeal, flour, baking powder, salt, baking soda, and black pepper in large bowl.
5. In medium bowl, whisk together yogurt, egg, egg whites, sugar, and remaining 1/4 c oil.
6. Fold in bell pepper mixture and corn. Fold into dry Ingredients: until just moistened.

7. DIVIDE batter evenly among prepared muffin cups. Bake 25 to 30 minutes or until wooden pick inserted in center comes out clean.
8. Cool in pan on wire rack 5 minutes. Remove muffins from pan to cool completely on wire rack.

Hearty Roast Beef Panini

Ingredients:

- 1/4 avocado, sliced

- 1/8 cup baby arugula

- 1 tsp Dijon mustard

- 2 slices reduced-calorie multigrain bread

- 2 ounces store-roasted, deli-sliced lean roast beef

- 2 beefsteak tomato slices

- 1/4 tsp extra virgin olive oil

- 2 cloves garlic, minced

- 1/4 cup soy sauce

- 2 tbsp hoisin sauce

- 1 tbsp honey

- 1 tsp cornstarch
- 2 tbsp vegetable oil
- 1 lb boneless, skinless chicken breast, sliced into thin strips
- 2 cups broccoli florets
- 1 red bell pepper, sliced
- 1 yellow onion, sliced
- Salt and pepper to taste

DIRECTIONS:

1. In a small bowl, mix together the soy sauce, hoisin sauce, honey, and cornstarch to make the sauce.
2. Heat the vegetable oil in a large skillet over medium-high heat.
3. Add the sliced chicken to the skillet and season with salt and pepper. Cook for 5-7

minutes, or until browned and cooked through.
4. Add the garlic to the skillet and cook for 1-2 minutes, or until fragrant.
5. Add the broccoli, red bell pepper, and onion to the skillet and stir to combine.
6. Pour the sauce over the chicken andvegetables and stir to coat.
7. Cook for 3-5 minutes, or until the vegetables are tender-crisp and the sauce has thickened.
8. Serve hot over rice or noodles and enjoy your delicious chicken and broccoli stir-fry.

Greek Salad with Grilled Chicken

Ingredients:

- 1/2 cup cherry tomatoes, halved
- 1/4 cup Kalamata olives
- 1/2 cup crumbled feta cheese
- 2 tbsp olive oil
- 1 tbsp red wine vinegar
- 1 tsp dried oregano
- 2 boneless, skinless chicken breasts
- 1 head romaine lettuce, chopped
- 1/2 cucumber, sliced
- 1/2 red onion, thinly sliced
- 1/2 red bell pepper, sliced
- Salt and pepper to taste

DIRECTIONS:

1. Preheat a grill or grill pan to medium-high heat.
2. Season the chicken breasts with salt and pepper and brush them with olive oil.
3. Grill the chicken for 5-7 minutes per side, or until cooked through.
4. Let the chicken rest for 5 minutes, then slice it into thin strips.
5. In a large bowl, combine the romaine lettuce, cucumber, red onion, red bell pepper, cherry tomatoes, and Kalamata olives.
6. In a small bowl, whisk together the olive oil, red wine vinegar, dried oregano, salt, and pepper to make the dressing.
7. Pour the dressing over the salad and toss to coat.
8. Add the sliced grilled chicken to the salad and sprinkle with crumbled feta cheese.

9. Serve immediately and enjoy your delicious Greek salad with grilled chicken.

Tuna Salad with Veggies and Hummus

Ingredients:

- 2 cans of tuna, drained
- 1/2 red onion, finely chopped
- 1/2 red bell pepper, finely chopped
- 1/2 cup cherry tomatoes, halved
- 1/4 cup chopped fresh parsley
- 1/4 cup hummus
- 1 tbsp Dijon mustard
- 1 tbsp lemon juice
- Salt and pepper to taste
- Mixed greens or lettuce for serving

DIRECTIONS:

1. In a large bowl, combine the tuna, red onion, red bell pepper, cherry tomatoes, and parsley.
2. In a small bowl, whisk together the hummus, Dijon mustard, lemon juice, salt, and pepper to make the dressing.
3. Pour the dressing over the tuna mixture and stir until well combined.
4. Serve the tuna salad over a bed of mixed greens or lettuce.

Baked Salmon with Roasted Vegetables

Ingredients:

- 1 zucchini, sliced

- 1 red onion, sliced

- 4 garlic cloves, minced

- 3 tbsp olive oil

- Salt and pepper to taste

- 4 salmon fillets

- 1 bunch asparagus, trimmed

- 1 red bell pepper, seeded and sliced

- 1 yellow squash, sliced

- Lemon wedges for serving

DIRECTIONS:

1. Preheat the oven to 400°F (200°C).

2. Arrange the asparagus, red bell pepper, yellow squash, zucchini, red onion, and garlic on a large baking sheet.
3. Drizzle the vegetables with olive oil and season with salt and pepper to taste.
4. Toss the vegetables to coat evenly with the oil and spices.
5. Bake the vegetables for 20-25 minutes, or until tender and lightly browned.
6. Season the salmon fillets with salt and pepper.
7. Place the salmon fillets on the baking sheet with the roasted vegetables.
8. Drizzle the salmon fillets with olive oil and bake for 12-15 minutes, or until the salmon is cooked through.
9. Serve the baked salmon and roasted vegetables with lemon wedges.

Smoothie with Tropical Kale and Greens

Ingredients:

- 1 avocado (medium)
- ¼ lemon peel
- 1 tbsp. sliced ginger with a grain of salt
- 1 cup of fresh kale leaves
- 1 apple, medium size
- ½ cup pure water

DIRECTIONS:

1. Rinse the kale under running water. Pull separate the leaves.
2. Core and slice apples without peeling.
3. Cut the avocado in half, remove the seed, and scoop out the flesh with a tablespoon.
4. Peel the lemon and remove the seeds.
5. Peel and thinly slice the ginger.

6. Combine all of the Ingredients: in a blender. Whiz on high until fully combined and smooth.
7. Serve in a large glass and enjoy!

Summer Salad Smoothie

Ingredients:

- ½ tiny avocados

- ½ cup sliced cucumber

- ½ lime fruit juice

- ½ cup pure water

- 10 mint leaves

- 10 leaves of sweet basil

- 10 coriander leaves

- 2 cups chunked watermelon

DIRECTIONS:

1. Remove the seeds from the watermelon before slicing them into slices. Scoop out the avocado fruit's flesh. Cucumbers should be cut into half-inch slices.

2. In a blender, combine the following Ingredients: in the following order: mint, basil, coriander, water, watermelon, avocado, cucumber, and lime juice. Mix until smooth on high speed.
3. Pour into a large glass and serve.

Ginger Water Recipe Flat Belly Diet

INGREDIENTS:

- 1 liter water - plain drinking

- 2 inch ginger root - knob, fresh

- 1 lemon - large

DIRECTIONS:

1. In a large glass jar add in plain water, peeled and grated ginger root and sliced lemons.
2. Stir in all the additions into the water so that they don't settle at the bottom of the jar.
3. Cover the jar with a lid and allow this water to be infused with all the goodness of the ginger and lemons.
4. Allow to steep at least for 6 hours, but overnight is preferred. You may refrigerate the jar of water as well.

5. The next morning pour out the water into a drinking glass, and drink instead of plain water or high calorie sodas.
6. You can use the same Ingredients: by changing the water two times, after which, discard the grated ginger and lemon slices and make a fresh batch.
7. Your ginger water recipe flat belly diet is ready.

VIETNAMESE BEEF SALAD

INGREDIENTS:

- 2 teaspoons chili paste

- 1/2 lb flank steak

- 6 cups mixed greens

- 1 cup sweet basil

- 1 cup cilantro leaf

- 1 red onion, thinly sliced (about 1 1/4 cups)

- 2 large English seedless cucumbers, with peel, julienned (about 4 c)

- 4 medium carrots, julienned (about2c)

- 1/4 cup soy sauce, reduced sodium

- 1/4 cup lime juice

- 1/4 cup water

- 2 tablespoons sugar

- 1 tablespoon garlic, minced

- 1/2 cup dry-roasted unsalted peanuts (MUFA, chopped)

DIRECTIONS:

1. COMBINE soy sauce, lime juice, water, sugar, garlic, and chile paste in medium bowl. Whisk to blend. Pour 3 tablespoons into a resealable plastic bag. Cover and refrigerate the remaining dressing. Add steak to bag, seal, and turn to coat. Chill 30 minutes to marinate.

2. HEAT grill or broiler to medium-high heat. Grill steak 8 to 10 minutes, turning once, or until medium-rare. Let rest 5 minutes and slice thinly at an angle, across the grain.

3. PLACE greens, basil, and cilantro in large bowl and toss. Evenly divide mixture among 4 plates. Sprinkle on onion, cucumbers, and carrots. Top with sliced steak, drizzle salad

with reserved dressing, and sprinkle with peanuts.

Blueberry-Pomegranate Juice

Ingredients:

- 120ml of water

- 1 tablespoon of honey

- 1/2 lemon (juiced)

- 150g of frozen blueberries

- 85g of pomegranate seeds

DIRECTIONS:

1. Place the frozen blueberries, pomegranate seeds, water, honey, and lemon juice in a juicer.
2. Juice on high speed until all the Ingredients: are well amalgamate and the mixture is uniform.
3. Adjust sweetness and taste by adding more honey, if desired.

4. Use a fine-mesh sieve to strain the juice and remove any pulp or seeds.
5. Serve chilled and enjoy.

Grapefruit-Cucumber Juice

Ingredients:

- 250g of grapefruit
- 250g of fresh cucumber
- 120ml of water
- Ice cubes (as desired)

Directions:

1. Prepare the grapefruit by peeling and segmenting it, removing any seeds.
2. Peel and dice the cucumber.
3. In a juicer, combine the peeled grapefruit segments, diced cucumber, and water.
4. Juice on high speed until the compound is uniform and well combined.
5. If desired, add ice cubes.
6. Pour the juice into glasses and serve immediately.

Cali Khichi

INGREDIENTS:

- 1/2 cup green bell pepper diced
- 1/2 cup orange bell pepper diced
- 1/4 cup celery diced
- 1 medium jalapeno minced
- 1 teaspoon ginger root grated
- 1/2 teaspoon coriander powder
- 1/2 teaspoon cumin powder
- 1/2 teaspoon turmeric powder
- 1/2 teaspoon black pepper
- 1/2 teaspoon sea salt
- 1/4 cup pine nuts
- 1/2 cup fresh cilantro leaves chopped

- 2 large artichokes steamed

- 1 large lemon halved

- 2 1/2 cups vegetable broth

- 2 tablespoon olive oil

- 1/4 cup mung beans

- 1/2 cup black rice

- 1/2 cup onion diced

DIRECTIONS:

1. Heat oil in large pot until sizzling, add onions, bell peppers, celery, jalapeno, ginger and garlic until fragrant, about 3 minutes, then add spices stirring and allowing the aromatics to bloom (bring out their full flavor), about 3 minutes.
2. Add rice and mung beans, stir and then add the vegetable broth. Bring to a boil, cover,

reduce flame to medium and simmer for 18 to 20 minutes.
3. Stir in pine nuts, pumpkin seeds and cilantro. Serve in dishes or for grander presentation, serve in a steamed artichoke.

Fat Flush Soup Recipe

INGREDIENTS:

- 1 tablespoon olive oil

- 1 lb. ground turkey, lean (454 grams)

- 1 green bell pepper, chopped

- 1 yellow bell pepper, chopped

- 2 cups onion, chopped

- 1 lb. zucchini, chopped (454 grams)

- 10 ounces baby portabella mushrooms, chopped (283 grams)

- 3 cloves garlic, finely chopped

- 46 ounces V8 Spicy Hot vegetable juice (1.36 liters; low-sodium)

- 15 ounces canned kidney beans, drained (425 grams)

- 14.5 ounces diced tomatoes (canned) (411 grams; no salt added variety)

- 1 lime, juiced

- 1 tablespoon cumin

- 1 teaspoon coriander

- ¼ cup fresh parsley, finely chopped (curly or Italian parsley is fine)

- ¼ cup cilantro, finely chopped

- 2 medium jalapenos, chopped (remove seeds for less heat)

- 3 scallions, sliced (optional, for garnish)

DIRECTIONS:

1. Start by prepping your veggies! Chop the sweet peppers, onion, zucchini, mushrooms, garlic, parsley, cilantro, jalapenos, and slice the scallions.

2. Heat the olive oil in a Dutch oven or another large pot over medium heat. Add the turkey, yellow pepper, green pepper, onion, zucchini, mushrooms, and garlic. Cook until the turkey is browned, stirring frequently. It will take approximately 20 minutes.
3. Add the rest of the ingredients to the pot, aside from the scallions. Heat to a simmer, stirring occasionally. It will take about 15 minutes.
4. Ladle the soup into bowls (or meal prep containers) and garnish with scallions. Wasn't that easy?

www.ingramcontent.com/pod-product-compliance
Lightning Source LLC
LaVergne TN
LVHW010224070526
838199LV00062B/4718